Put Beginning Readers on the Right Track with
ALL ABOARD READING™

The All Aboard Reading series is especially for beginning readers. Written by noted authors and illustrated in full color, these are books that children really and truly *want* to read—books to excite their imagination, tickle their funny bone, expand their interests, and support their feelings. With four different reading levels, All Aboard Reading lets you choose which books are most appropriate for your children and their growing abilities.

Picture Readers—for Ages 3 to 6
Picture Readers have super-simple texts, with many nouns appearing as rebus pictures. At the end of each book are 24 flash cards—on one side is the rebus picture; on the other side is the written-out word.

Level 1—for Preschool through First-Grade Children
Level 1 books have very few lines per page, very large type, easy words, lots of repetition, and pictures with visual "cues" to help children figure out the words on the page.

Level 2—for First-Grade to Third-Grade Children
Level 2 books are printed in slightly smaller type than Level 1 books. The stories are more complex, but there is still lots of repetition in the text, and many pictures. The sentences are quite simple and are broken up into short lines to make reading easier.

Level 3—for Second-Grade through Third-Grade Children
Level 3 books have considerably longer texts, harder words, and more complicated sentences.

All Aboard for happy reading!

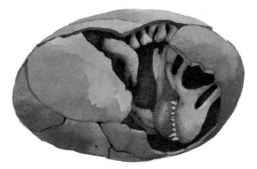

Dedicated to Imani—P.J.

Text copyright © 2000 by Jennifer Dussling. Illustrations copyright © 2000 by Pamela Johnson. All rights reserved. Published by Grosset & Dunlap, a division of Penguin Putnam Books for Young Readers, New York. GROSSET & DUNLAP and ALL ABOARD READING are trademarks of Penguin Putnam Inc. Published simultaneously in Canada. Printed in the U.S.A.

Library of Congress Cataloging-in-Publication Data is available.

ISBN 0-448-42093-7 (pb)   A B C D E F G H I J
ISBN 0-448-42094-5 (GB)   A B C D E F G H I J

ALL
ABOARD
READING™

Level 2
Grades 1-3

Dinosaur Eggs

By Jennifer Dussling
Illustrated by Pamela Johnson

Grosset & Dunlap • New York

The jeep turned
and then pulled to a stop.
The people in the jeep
were fossil hunters.

They were searching for fossils of birds

from dinosaur times.

They hoped to find

a fossil, or two, or three.

They never imagined

how lucky they would be.

The fossil hunters stepped down

from the jeep.

They looked around.

They saw what looked like

many round rocks.

Each one was the size of a grapefruit.

One of the fossil hunters

took a closer look.

He gasped.

The rocks were fossil eggs.

But they were not bird eggs.

They were dinosaur eggs!

There were thousands of them!

The team had found

a dinosaur nesting ground!

For fossil hunters,

this was like striking gold.

Some of these eggs still

had baby dinosaurs inside them!

The babies had never hatched.

They had become fossils.

During the next few weeks,

the team found dozens

of baby dinosaurs in eggs.

Some babies even had skin.

No one had ever found that before!

There were fossils of

little skulls and leg bones.

One egg held thirty-two tiny teeth.

What did the fossil hunters

learn from these eggs?

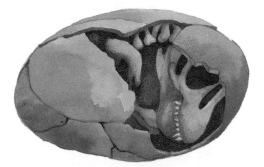

Stegosaurus

Tyrannosaurus Rex

Compsognathus

Now they knew that

these were sauropod eggs.

(You say it like this: SORE-oh-pod.)

Sauropod

Sauropods were the largest dinosaurs ever to walk the Earth.

Sauropods had long necks and long tails.

They weighed up to thirty tons.

That's as much as twenty elephants.

Sauropods were huge,

but they were not fierce.

They ate only plants.

Sauropods traveled in groups.

Young dinosaurs traveled with

grown-up ones.

The grown-ups protected them

from meat-eating enemies.

How did scientists figure that out?

They looked at tracks.

The big footprints of sauropods
showed they walked together.

Now fossil hunters saw that

sauropods nested in groups, too.

The nesting ground proved that.

The sauropods waited
at the same place
for their babies to hatch.

Together the big dinosaurs
fought off meat-eaters.
The meat-eaters could not
get to the eggs.

These eggs were from a type

of sauropod called titanosaur.

(You say it like this: TY-tan-oh-sore.)

Titanic means big. Some titanosaurs
grew to be over fifty feet long.
That's longer than a tractor trailer!

But titanosaurs started small.

They were only fifteen inches long

at birth.

They did not stay tiny for long.

Titanosaur babies grew quickly.

They grew to full size

in eight to ten years.

That's some growth spurt!

Growing fast was important

for young dinosaurs.

Small babies were often in danger.

Other dinosaurs might eat them.

Scientists discovered something else
that was interesting.
Grown-up titanosaurs
had bony plates in their skin,
like a crocodile.

But the baby titanosaurs
in the eggs didn't.
Their skin was bumpy
like a football.

So now scientists knew
the plates must have grown
after the babies hatched.

So, why didn't these babies hatch
from these eggs?
What happened
at the nesting ground?

This nesting ground was by a river.

Around eighty million years ago,

a huge group of titanosaurs nested there.

These dinosaurs ate
the leaves and needles
from high trees.

The big dinosaurs also
watch over their eggs.

These eggs were very
close to hatching.

All of a sudden,

the river was overflowing!

A flood of water and mud

washed over the nesting ground.

The large titanosaurs ran away.

They had to leave their eggs.

The nesting ground was covered

by mud and dirt.

None of the eggs could hatch.

The mud seeped into tiny holes

in the eggshells.

Mud covered the baby dinosaurs.

No air could get inside the eggs.

This kept the skin and bones

of the babies from rotting.

After many, many years, the eggs—

and the babies inside them—

became fossils.

And millions of years after that,

a jeep with fossil hunters

drove up to the nesting ground.

And they made a wonderful discovery.

There are still many facts that

the dinosaur hunters hope to learn.

Did titanosaurs bring food to their babies?

Did they keep their eggs warm?

But what the team found that day
has changed what we know
about sauropods.
Museums will need to fix their displays.

The fossil hunters

will come back to the nesting ground.

There are still thousands of eggs

to look at.

There probably are

more baby dinosaurs

in some of those eggs.

Who knows

what other dinosaur secrets

are hidden in that rocky land?